Black Muslim Wife & Husband

By Rasheed L. Muhammad

Proverbs 25:11

"Like apples of gold in settings of silver, is a word spoken in right circumstances"

Book Key
Definitions

Console: the act or an instance of consoling
:the state of being consoled: comfort:

Husband: married man: male head of a
household:

Heaven: a blissful place of existence:

Mind: the element of a person that enables them
to be aware of the world and their experiences,
to think, and to feel; the faculty of
consciousness and thought:

Civilized: bring (a place or people) to a stage of
social, cultural, and moral development
considered to be more
advanced:

Provide: make available for use; supply:

Icy: (of a person's tone or manner) very
unfriendly; hostile:

Hell: a place or state of misery, torment, or wickedness:

Submit: to yield to governance or authority:

Recognize: to acknowledge with a show of appreciation:

Train: teach (a person) a particular skill or type of behavior through practice and instruction over a period of time:

Wife: veiled person[1]: A wife is a female partner in a continuing marital relationship:

---

[1] http://etymonline.com/index.php?term=wife

Contents

How a Women Keeps her Man Consoled

The Honorable Elijah Muhammad is the founding father of the Nation of Islam in the West. He is the spiritual father of the Honorable Minister Louis Farrakhan and many other men and women both known and unknown. His message reformed some the worst Black men and women of North America into some of the best. Today what makes his nation outstanding among 40 to 60 million Black people in North America is his teaching that good wife and husband accept in patience and prayer.

Along these same lines, The Honorable Elijah Muhammad stated December 1967:

"I have Sister Frances teaching the sisters, and seeing how they cook in the kitchen. I want to see what they have learned. I say you are in class to learn how to take care of home, cooking and taking care of your husbands.

"A man has no better heaven than a wife, and if he has no heaven there, there is no heaven. Heaven begins in the home.

"A man is like an ox trying to go out and pull a cart to get something to eat. Yet you will find some of our women will treat the ox better. She would give it a pat on the back.

"<u>A wife's mind should be to console her husband's mind.</u>

"We want to prepare better men and women to be wives and husbands.

"A Woman is the only heaven a man has. Our Saviour said this and said the woman must honor the man and must obey him.

"A man and woman are like twins before marriage and after marriage are one. Man and woman are part of each other, flesh and blood. Holy Quran states you are created one of each other.

The Saviour says, 'Brother we control the woman, we are the boss. If you want her to obey you, keep her in the house. If you don't keep her under control she is dangerous. We don't trust her.

"Satan ruins the woman. He does not want her shut in, but on display. She is hard to train. What is woman for? We got her to work for her and for her to console you. She is to do something in the way of making you feel good to go out tomorrow to work. Otherwise, man is outside looking for peace of mind.

"No man wants a woman home arguing with him. I'm telling you the truth. I know by experience. Man does not care if he satisfies her or not. He has no spirit for it.

"Woman, speak a good word for him, whether he works hard or not. Console him. Respect him. When we learn better, we should do better.

"Man should not wreck the peace of the home by arguing. He should tell her by not acting savage. Don't depart from each other without letting the other know. Be civilized in asking and telling. That's right acting. The man in Islam must change. We must treat her right and we must make her treat us right.

"Give her what she needs. Provide for her. Tell her if she wants to see what's out, I'll take you around.

"What does a wife look like telling her husband she has a right to go because he *goes? The man always goes out looking as a provider for his wife and family. What does a man look like taking care of a woman who goes where she pleases? She should go where he pleases and it pleases him. The Holy Quran teaches "one is an enemy to each other for they are divided".*

"Keep up the happy spirit in the home. Again the woman is to be a consoler in every way; mends his clothes. She is to work to try to please you. Then you'll try to work to please her. This is for all of us.

"Newly married and those who have been married. Islam is a peaceful religion. When you become one, one can be one. If you have to take away from one you must turn it into a fraction. If you have become one you should think in terms of one and work in the interest of one.

"Man and wife in Islam are one. She works to please her husband and he works to please her when he knows he has that kind of wife. God is one, the religion is one and man and wife are one. One and One. Woman must do her part as a wife. Birth

children, nurse them and have a peaceful home. This is Islam.

"We were savages yesterday. Let us be civilized today. Birds show good examples of love toward each other.

"The worst hell is an icy spirit between husband and wife in a home where there is no peace, no love. This is hell, where two don't want each other.

"A wise human being who has vision should show more sense than that animal who has no vision. Then, God can smile saying I extend peace to them and they have peace. The Holy Quran states, 'I have adjusted your affairs adjustable.' And I say to you, nothing is more pleasing than to have peace at home daily.

"The Holy Quran states if you can't get along, I permit you to divorce, but it is not the way of the Lord.

"Settle down to a good choice, settle down to one who will bring you peace and contentment. Don't speculate; if you can't get along, go. When you come to an agreement, don't pick up embers of it and throw it into a new disagreement.

"We must learn to live in peace or live out of it. A man and woman are made to make peace for each other that makes peace for a nation.

Woman must always submit and recognize man as the head. Even if the husband is a junky husband yet he is the man. By nature man can't submit to the woman.

"The Holy Quran says woman has equal rights as he has rights over her, but these rights are defined. We are talking about rights now, not authority. Rights are not authority. The Holy Quran says he is exalted over you. He is the sustainer over you. He is the authority and woman is subject to the authority.

"Love makes us humble to the law. If we love each we won't disagree. When you love someone, you love them for yourself.

"It's the woman who is the 2nd self. Man is the 1st self. When first life germ created in darkness it brought itself into being and became a light of himself and from himself he produced a sphere and mattered it into matter. How could man be

a self-light? We need that which gives off a light and the lightning bug is in their own light. The God did that to give you a sign. Jehovah made Moses' skin to shine. Electric is in the light and the light is part of us and we created that sun but the sun did not create us. We are self-created. Since you can't find the end of light, you can't find the end of God. If you can't understand the source of light you can't understand the source of God. Thank you

Consoling Words of Wife to Husband

33

It is ever so obvious that we (male and female) both need attention from one another? Let us stay away from negative attention lest we make fools of ourselves.

Wife in Jewish History

The Holy Quran 30:21 says, *"Among His proofs is that He created for you spouses from among yourselves, in order to have tranquility and contentment with each other, and He placed in your hearts love and care towards your spouses. In this, there are sufficient proofs for people who think."* But today's society is dominated by male egotism that has led to female narcissism, boob and booty worship.

Consequently, millions of husbands and wives are besieged with self-absorbance, money worship and materialism merely to keep up with "the jones". For those not familiar with this phrase, it originates with the comic strip *Keeping Up with the Joneses*, created by Arthur R. "Pop" Momand in 1913. The strip ran until 1940 in *The New York World* and various other newspapers. The strip depicts the social climbing McGinis family, who struggle to "keep up" with their neighbors, the Joneses...[2] I imagine the wife of Mr. Jones was very much provided for and Mr. McGinis was under pressure to make his wife feel just as secure that he too could provide her earthly needs, wants and desires.

The Bible lays out a series of verses and passages regarding the role between husband and wife, the nucleus of our original family unit. Nevertheless, do women get disappointed reading Biblical and Quranic verses and passages prescribing male and female roles?

For instance: **Wife:** The duties of husbands and wives in their relations to each other are distinctly set forth in the New Testament (1 Corinthians 7:2-5; Ephesians 5:22-33; Colossians 3:18 Colossians 3:19 ; 1 Peter 3:1-7).

---

[2] https://en.wikipedia.org/wiki/Keeping_up_with_the_Joneses

[However], the ordinance of marriage was sanctioned in Paradise (Genesis 2:24; Matthew 19:4-6). Monogamy was the original law under which man lived, but polygamy early commenced (Genesis 4:19), and continued to prevail all down through Jewish history.

The Law of Moses regulated but did not prohibit polygamy. A man might have a plurality of wives, but a wife could have only one husband.

A wife's legal rights (Exodus 21:10) and her duties (Proverbs 31:10-31 ; 1 Timothy 5:14) are specified. She could be divorced in special cases (Deuteronomy 22:13-21), but could not divorce her husband. Divorce was restricted by our Lord to the single case of adultery (Matthew 19:3-9). Of course, women do not want to deal with this today because men and/or husbands have gone far off the right path. The lawlessness of the land in dealing with rights and authority with respect to husband and wife has become a conundrum. It is as if people, small and great, do not think anymore except to refute, refute and refute more simply to remain in bubbles of narcissism—pursuit of gratification from vanity or egotistic admiration of one's own attributes.[3] In the end, these two personalities pass on into self-protective strategies i.e., *"an icy spirit between husband and wife in a home where there is no peace, no love. This is hell, where two don't want each other."*[4]

Or is it that women get disappointed in the actions or lack of action by men regarding their ideal or imagined relationship? I know, the male and female dynamic is a mystery for far too many of us to remain as the Quran states, *'I have adjusted your affairs adjustable.'*

---

[3] http://www.biblestudytools.com/dictionary/wife/
[4] Hon. Elijah Muhammad page. 10 "My Wife Knows Everything".

Women and God

The Nation of Islam is the only nation that officially publicizes that woman is the second self of God. Her power of attraction is almost so irresistible to man that he sometimes goes crazy over her. But why? What secrets does she hold in her nature to attract man?

Mother Tynnetta Muhammad divulged:

"The Most Honorable Elijah Muhammad taught us in his magnificent lecture series, "The Theology of Time," and in private discussions and in his books that the attracting power of the Sun is so terrific that she is referred to in the feminine gender. When examining the word "feminine," we have inside

the word "min" (men) and the number "nine."

"This aspect of the "feminine" in God reflects the power of the female as co-creator with her attracting power to procreate and produce offspring which is symbolized in the creation of the nine planets orbiting around the Sun. This seminal act of creation produces the different civilizations existing on each of our planets in our solar system. This is the Secret Power of the female, the Mother, the Second Self of God, as Co-creator and co-Producer of life repeated over and over again.

"Why is the Sun identified as "she" in the Arabic language? And why are all planets and their kingdoms, including all-star systems, referred to as "she" in the feminine gender? And why does the Most Honorable Elijah Muhammad place *emphasis on our Sun as "she"? What might the Secret of God, held as a secret for trillions of years, have to do with this feminine aspect of the Divine Creation?*

"The Honorable Minister Louis Farrakhan has taught us that the Secret of God lies in the woman. This means that the True Knowledge of God and the True Knowledge of self cannot be understood without the woman, the female, Second Self of God, coming from the Divine Word of God in giving birth to a New World Civilization and Kingdom of Peace with unlimited progress, Freedom, Justice and Equality for all, irrespective of gender.[5]

---

[5] http://www.finalcall.com/artman/publish/Columns_4/article_101427.shtml

Problem 13

In the Nation of Islam, there are a total of 154 questions and answers contained in there Supreme Book of Wisdom. These lessons were captured by the FBI during the early 1940's when they arrested Elijah Muhammad for teaching Islam.

Of all the lessons, Problem 13 is the only one mentioned twice. It is as followers:

"13. After learning Mathematics, which is Islam, and Islam is Mathematics, it stands true. You can always prove it at no limit of time. Then you must learn to use it and secure some benefit while you are living, that is- luxury, money, good homes, friendship in all walks of life.

"Sit yourself in Heaven at once! This is the greatest Desire of your Brother and Teachers.

"Now you must speak the language so you can use your Mathematical Theology

in the proper Term - otherwise you will not be successful unless you do speak well, for she knows all about you.

"The Secretary of Islam offers a reward to the best and neatest worker of this Problem.

"There are twenty-six letters in the Language and if a student learns one letter per day, then how long will it take him to learn the twenty-six letters?

"There are ten numbers in the Mathematical Language. Then how long will it take a Student to learn the whole ten numbers (at the above rate)?

"The average man speaks four hundred words - considered well."

Of course the lack of math and language skills is what the enemy of the black nation. However, the fundamental and best way to interpret **Problem 13** is for both husband and wife, male and female, to re-evaluate pages *8 – 14* of this book again.

What you may discover s that a major part of the solution between male and female (husband and wife) rest in what the Honorable Elijah Muhammad commissioned Dear Sister Frances teach the sisters during the 1960's.

Heaven Lies at the Foot of Mother

"*Heaven Lies at the Foot of Mother.*" This quotation was spoken by Prophet Muhammad, Ibn Abdullah, 1,400 years ago in his great work of reform and civilizing of the Arab people in the days of their ignorance. This quotation is applicable to us as well today. Heaven represents a state of peace where the citizens of heaven live in accordance with the laws, rules, statutes or commandments of Allah (God). This is also called in scripture the Kingdom of God. Again, it is called the

Min. Louis Farrakhan

hereafter. The Honorable Elijah Muhammad taught us that the hereafter means *here* on the earth *after* the works of Satan are destroyed..."

"...Would not you like to replace the hell that is on the earth with a heavenly life? Would you not like to see your children grow up in a more peaceful environment? What will you give to see such a heavenly state come into existence? The Honorable Elijah Muhammad said that, *"He would give all that He has and all within His power to see such a day when Satan's world will be destroyed and a better world come into existence...."*

"...*Heaven Lies at the Foot of Mother.* This means that we must help in the production of a righteous woman. As men, we must know that the little girls that come into this world come in pure and we as husbands, father, brothers, uncles and cousins must commit ourselves to protect the purity of females that we come in contact with, particularly fathers, uncles, and brothers, for, oft-times it is family members that are destroying the virtue of our young girls.